michael bublé
CALL ME IRRESPONSIBLE

ISBN 13: 978-1-4234-3200-5
ISBN 10: 1-4234-3200-2

HAL•LEONARD® CORPORATION
7777 W. BLUEMOUND RD. P.O. BOX 13819 MILWAUKEE, WI 53213

For all works contained herein:
Unauthorized copying, arranging, adapting, recording or public performance is an infringement of copyright.
Infringers are liable under the law.

Visit Hal Leonard Online at
www.halleonard.com

CONTENTS

ALWAYS ON MY MIND

Words and Music by WAYNE THOMPSON,
MARK JAMES and JOHNNY CHRISTOPHER

© 1971 (Renewed 1999), 1979 SCREEN GEMS-EMI MUSIC INC. and SEBANINE MUSIC, INC.
All Rights Controlled and Administered by SCREEN GEMS-EMI MUSIC INC.
All Rights Reserved   International Copyright Secured   Used by Permission

THE BEST IS YET TO COME

Music by CY COLEMAN
Lyrics by CAROLYN LEIGH

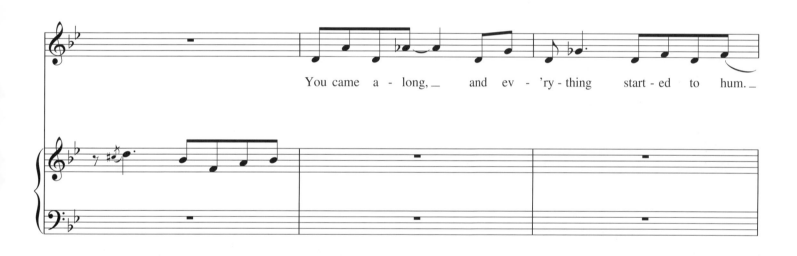

Copyright © 1959 Notable Music Company, Inc. and EMI Carwin Music Inc.
Copyright Renewed
All Rights for Notable Music Company, Inc. Administered by Chrysalis Music
All Rights Reserved   Used by Permission

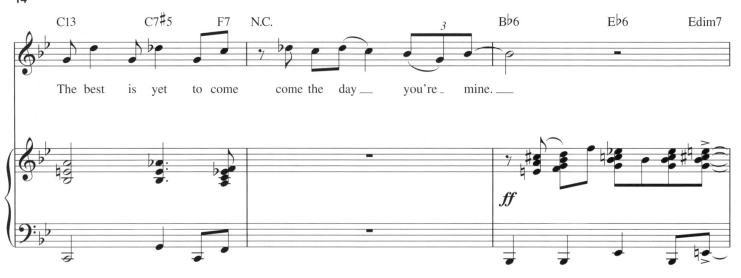

The best is yet to come come the day ___ you're ___ mine. ___

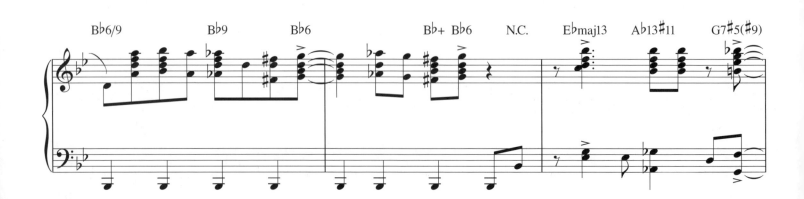

CALL ME IRRESPONSIBLE
from the Paramount Picture PAPA'S DELICATE CONDITION

Words by SAMMY CAHN
Music by JAMES VAN HEUSEN

*Recorded a half step higher.

Copyright © 1962, 1963 (Renewed 1990, 1991) by Paramount Music Corporation
International Copyright Secured   All Rights Reserved

ir – re – spon – si – bly mad for _____ you. _____

COMIN' HOME BABY

Words and Music by ROBERT DOROUGH
and BENJAMIN TUCKER

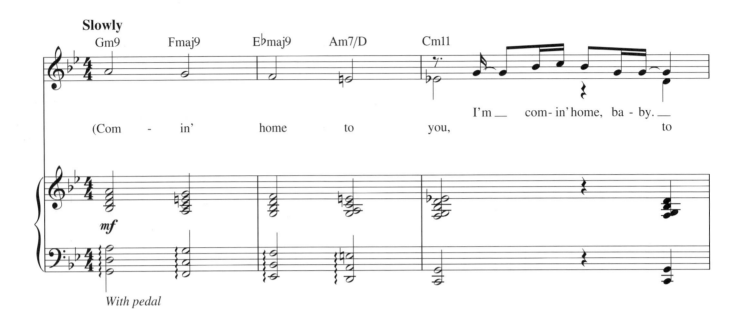

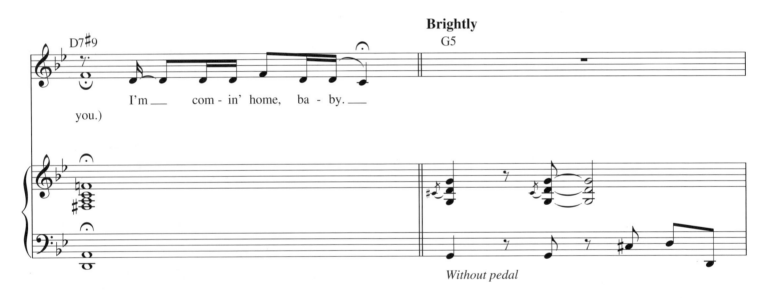

Copyright © 1962 SINCERE MUSIC CO. and BENGLO MUSIC INC.
Copyright Renewed
All Rights Controlled and Administered by IRVING MUSIC, INC.
All Rights Reserved   Used by Permission

28

G
right.
Please come home;
I'm press-in' on, ba-by, now.
Am
I wan-na feel you hold
I wan-na feel you hold
me tight.
C
B7
B♭7
me tight.
When I'm in your arms, I'll be
When I'm in your arms, I'll be
Am6
Am
Am(maj7)
fine.
fine.)
I'm com-in' home.
(Come on home;

DREAM

Words and Music by
JOHNNY MERCER

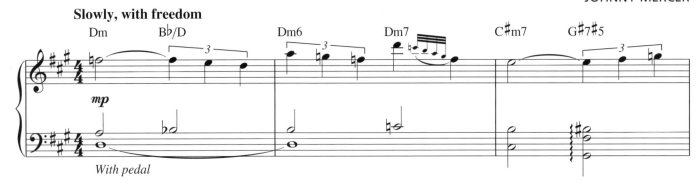

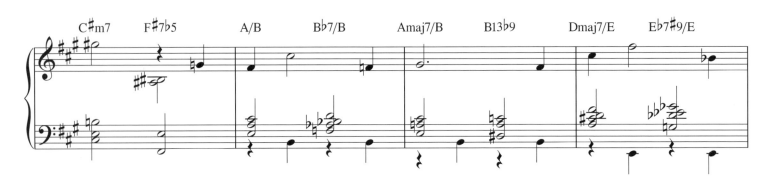

Dream _____ when you're feel-ing blue.

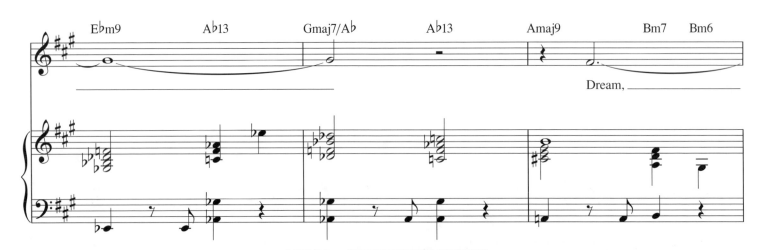

Dream, _____

© 1945 (Renewed) THE JOHNNY MERCER FOUNDATION
All Rights Administered by WB MUSIC CORP.
All Rights Reserved   Used by Permission

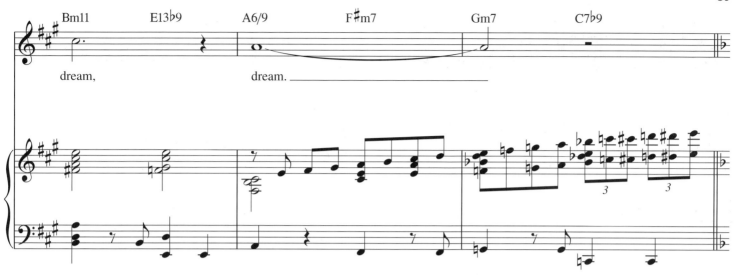

dream,

dream. _____

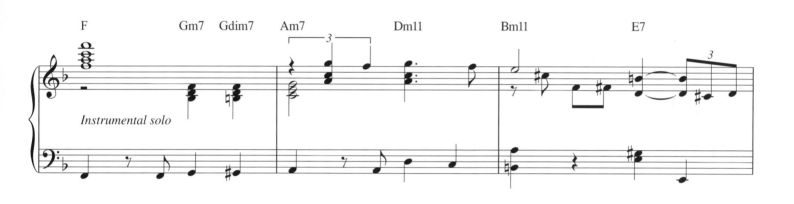

Instrumental solo

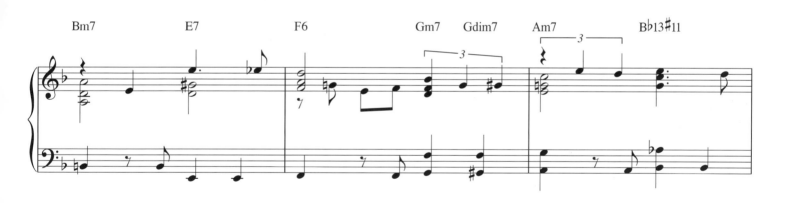

40

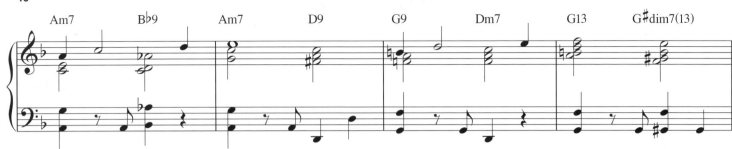

D.S. al Coda

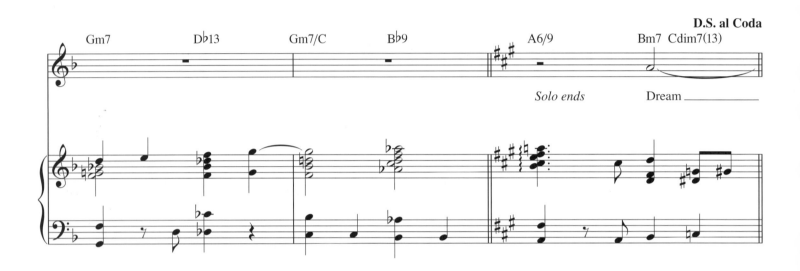

Solo ends   Dream _____

CODA

dream,   dream,   dream. _____

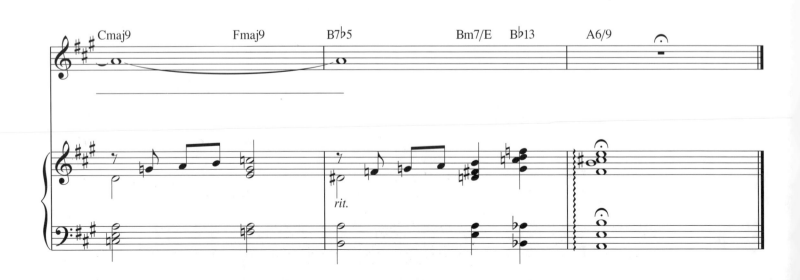

EVERYTHING

Words and Music by AMY FOSTER-GILLIES,
MICHAEL BUBLÉ and ALAN CHANG

User 1, E, 3
Voice/Master

Copyright © 2005 SONGS OF UNIVERSAL, INC., ALMOST OCTOBER SONGS, I'M THE LAST MAN STANDING MUSIC and IHAN ZHAN MUSIC
All Rights for ALMOST OCTOBER SONGS Controlled and Administered by SONGS OF UNIVERSAL, INC.
All Rights for I'M THE LAST MAN STANDING MUSIC Controlled and Administered by WB MUSIC CORP.
All Rights for IHAN ZHAN MUSIC Controlled and Administered by SONY/ATV MUSIC PUBLISHING, 8 Music Square West, Nashville, TN 37203
All Rights Reserved   Used by Permission

I'M YOUR MAN

Words and Music by
LEONARD COHEN

*Recorded a half step lower.

Copyright © 1988 Sony/ATV Songs LLC
All Rights Administered by Sony/ATV Music Publishing, 8 Music Square West, Nashville, TN 37203
International Copyright Secured   All Rights Reserved

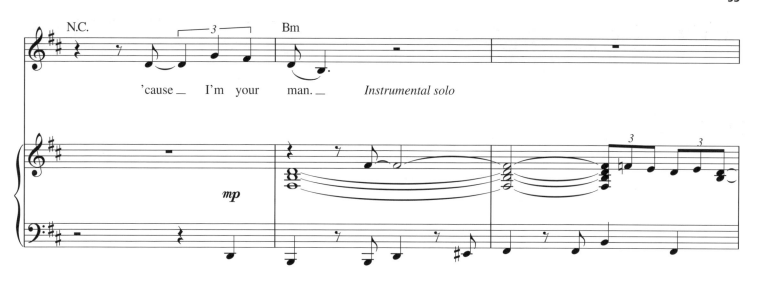

'cause ___ I'm your man. ___ *Instrumental solo*

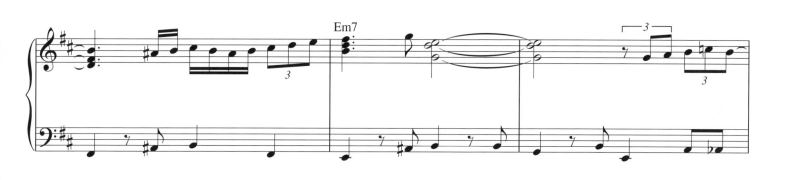

I'VE GOT THE WORLD ON A STRING

Lyric by TED KOEHLER
Music by HAROLD ARLEN

© 1932 (Renewed 1960) FRED AHLERT MUSIC GROUP, TED KOEHLER MUSIC CO./Administered by BUG MUSIC and S.A. MUSIC CO.
All Rights Reserved   Used by Permission

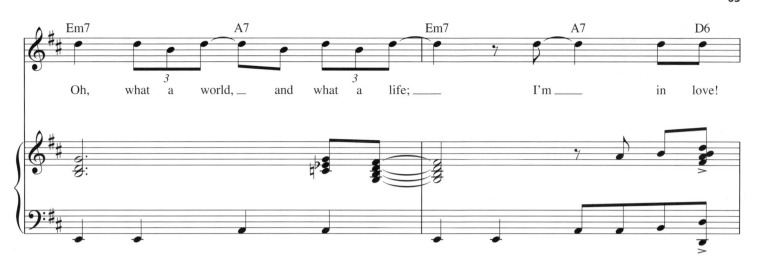

Oh, what a world, __ and what a life; ____ I'm ____ in love!

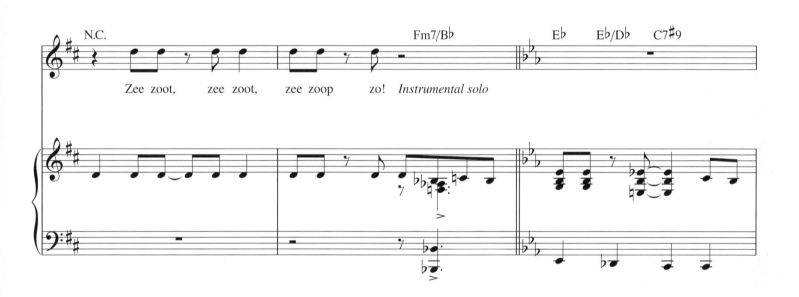

Zee zoot, zee zoot, zee zoop zo! *Instrumental solo*

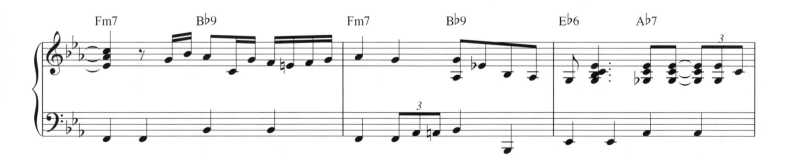

IT HAD BETTER BE TONIGHT

Music by HENRY MANCINI
English Lyrics by JOHNNY MERCER
Italian Lyrics by FRANCO MIGLIACCI

© 1962 (Renewed) NORTHRIDGE MUSIC COMPANY and EMI U CATALOG INC.
Exclusive Worldwide Print Rights Administered by ALFRED PUBLISHING CO., INC.
All Rights Reserved   Used by Permission

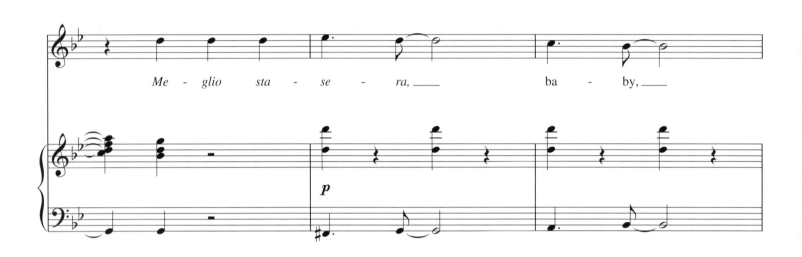

Me - glio sta - se - ra, _____ ba - by, _____

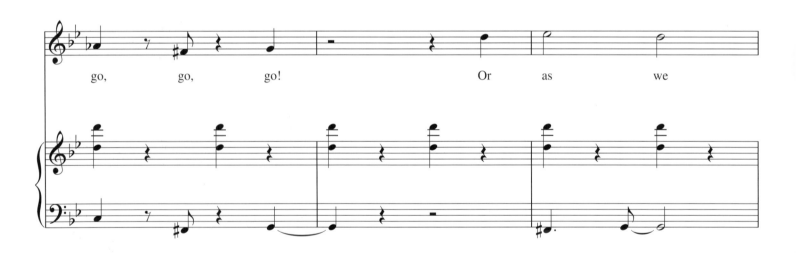

go, go, go! Or as we

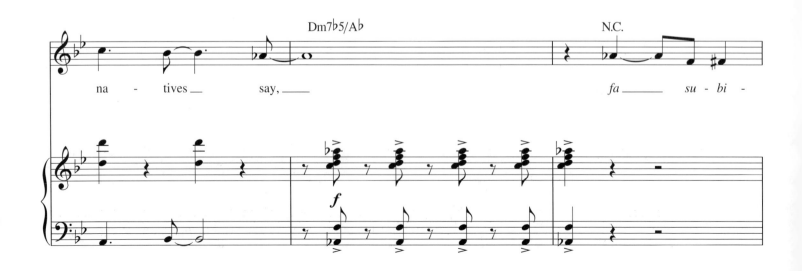

na - tives _____ say, _____ fa _____ su - bi -

LOST

Words and Music by JANN ARDEN RICHARDS,
MICHAEL BUBLÉ and ALAN CHANG

Recorded a half step lower.

Copyright © 2007 UNIVERSAL MUSIC PUBLISHING, A Division of UNIVERSAL MUSIC CANADA, INC., GIRL ON THE MOON MUSIC, I'M THE LAST MAN STANDING MUSIC and IHAN ZHAN MUSIC
All Rights for UNIVERSAL MUSIC PUBLISHING, A Division of UNIVERSAL MUSIC CANADA, INC. and GIRL ON THE MOON MUSIC in the United States and Canada
Controlled and Administered by UNIVERSAL - POLYGRAM INTERNATIONAL PUBLISHING, INC.
All Rights for I'M THE LAST MAN STANDING MUSIC Controlled and Administered by WB MUSIC CORP.
All Rights for IHAN ZHAN MUSIC Controlled and Administered by SONY/ATV MUSIC PUBLISHING, 8 Music Square West, Nashville, TN 37203
All Rights Reserved   Used by Permission

ME AND MRS. JONES

Words and Music by KENNETH GAMBLE,
LEON HUFF and CARY GILBERT

Moderately slow

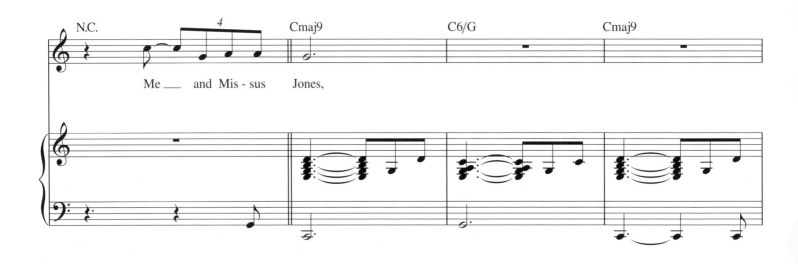

Me __ and Mis - sus Jones,

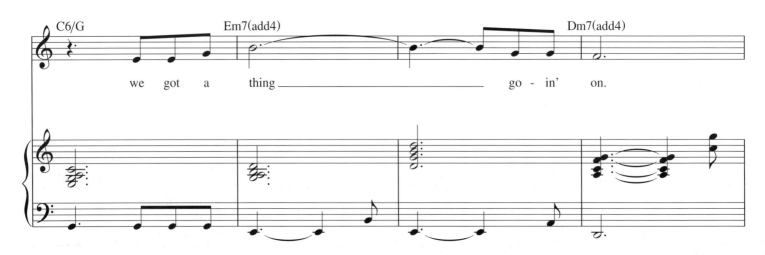

we got a thing __ go - in' on.

© 1973 (Renewed) WARNER-TAMERLANE PUBLISHING CORP.
All Rights Reserved   Used by Permissio

THAT'S LIFE

Words and Music by DEAN KAY
and KELLY GORDON

Don't __ let it get you, ____

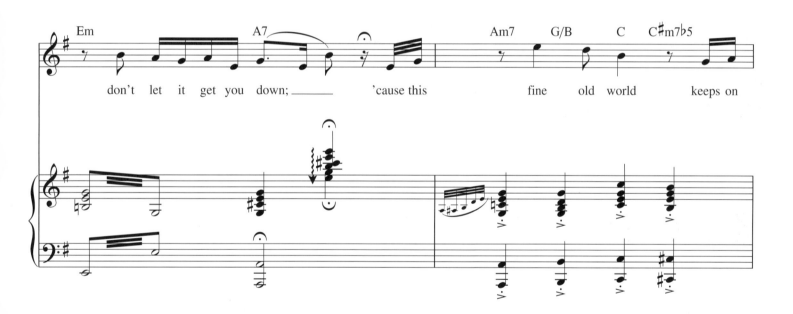

don't let it get you down; _____ 'cause this fine old world keeps on

spin - nin' 'round.

Copyright © 1964, 1966 UNIVERSAL - POLYGRAM INTERNATIONAL PUBLISHING, INC.
Copyright Renewed
All Rights Reserved   Used by Permission

WONDERFUL TONIGHT

Words and Music by
ERIC CLAPTON

Copyright © 1977 by Eric Patrick Clapton
Copyright Renewed
All Rights for the U.S. Administered by Unichappell Music Inc.
International Copyright Secured   All Rights Reserved

is that you just don't re - al - ize_____ how much I

love you.
Instrumental solo

Vocal ad lib.